Early Mourning Hours

Copyright © 2018 Samihah Pargas

Edited by Nakeysha Denace Roberts Washington
Cover design by Shabaaz Motala
and Ryan Wesley Green

I thank you all immensely.

Early Mourning Hours

Here? Or there?

"Everywhere."

Everywhere? What hurts everywhere?

"Every thing."

Why?

There was silence for a while, so I left my heart on the prayer mat.
I'd come back for it after the mourning.

Healing doesn't have a pretty face. It isn't consistent or casual.

You're more apart than altogether.

Redoing, rebuilding.

Pulling yourself out of skin too tight for you to wear any longer

dragging your body away from what kept hurting your heart

reshuffling the pieces.

Breaking down.

Rearranging. Maybe it'll work this time round, or maybe there are still a few thoughts out of place.

Necessary things still needing to be done in time you don't think you have.

Healing doesn't have a formula. It gives you back to yourself one piece at a time, or many pieces all at once. Sometimes you're so focused on how much more of yourself you must reclaim; you don't notice how much of yourself you've already found.

Healing is an oil lamp that runs on patience before its fire finally burns at its fullest.
And it will stun you every time, how softly the light seeps into your darkest hour.

Before you even think you're ready, there you go again with your renewed faith.

It will stun you every time
how it must undo your breath until you are able to breathe again.
It will lull your heart back into place with its hope, the moment that has you recognising the feel of happiness when it touches you after a while.

Healing needs time. It walks little footsteps that you never see yourself taking. You never see it coming. You are so busy waiting for it to happen in front of you. You don't notice when it starts inside.

"Something about dead roses," you say.
"It is as if they are the lovers who
although drained
continue to express love.
Continue to scent the skin with
sweet fragrance."

Is this why you love them so much?

Because they make you feel like you aren't the only one?

Visit.

Talk to me

or hold me.

We can be together

silent.

Don't say that you miss me

when I am near.

Early Mourning Hours

Your love was a part of their healing.

I wonder.

If only you could give it to yourself.

Early Mourning Hours

Waiting for someone
who will never love you
is not poetic.
It is damage. It
is long nights asking yourself why and
early mornings convincing yourself to stay
waiting for a thing that will never embrace you
the same way you embrace it
is pain. Longing. Frustration.
There is nothing poetic about hurting when the tears are
yours to cry.

Cry as much as it hurts
pray for longer than you've been waiting.

Break
and rebuild
and break again
but don't you stop walking my love.
With hardship comes ease.

— i. " *with* "

it is easier to excuse them
than it is to confront the pain they cause

it is easier to hold them
than to withhold from them

it is easier to starve yourself of love
than it is to deprive them of yours

it is easier.
because you are so accustomed to giving
that it feels selfish of you to
step back and let them be the
excuses.
and the holding and
the love
that you deserve.

Early Mourning Hours

That night I asked God to detach my heart from whatever was not written to be mine. I started forgetting about us. Gradually my mind learned to keep its distance from thoughts that once echoed your name. I wondered whether I was beginning to lose you or you, you were losing me. Later, I realised that slowly drifting away from you was that prayer being answered. It was Him taking my heart back from you before you could damage it.

I don't regret loving you. It taught me something I perhaps would not have learnt elsewhere.

I do, however, regret prioritising you before my Lord.

I loved you more and even then, He saved me.

Your love was yet to be found. You saw it in the dreams
you were chasing. With a heavy hand, I opened the door
for you and like a child, gazing–bewildered upon a
passing star, I watched you leave.
Perhaps what you were looking for was
very far away from me, but you'd be happy.

Our roads might part, turning us into mere memories of
each other
and that would simply be what had been predestined for
our souls. God only knows.
What I hope you remember of me is that

I love you enough
to have let you go.

Early Mourning Hours

It is easy to say
"do not accept anything less" than what you deserve
but sometimes you must be the one giving
instead of the one receiving.

— Laws of reciprocation

Early Mourning Hours

At times

closure cannot be given to you by anyone

does not appear in an apology

is not found in forgiveness

nor the ability to "forget".

At times

closure is felt only when we

are ready to *accept*.

— Accept the past for what it was and the present
for what it cannot be.

Early Mourning Hours

I have been to very dark places. I think you'd know
about darkness, always sharing your light while you
don't share your wars. Your heart is being torn apart in
silence. We are being torn apart too. I've stayed waiting
for you. Arms wide open. Smile through tears
nonetheless. But your back is turned. It's been turned for
a while. Talk to me. Tell me you're okay or tell me that
you're not. Tell me you need time to breathe or tell me
you want to be held. Lord knows how hard it is to
swallow your coldness, but you will still have my
warmth. You will always have my prayers. And even if
you throw our love away, I will find it for us. I will pick
it up. Dust it off. Keep it safe for when you decide to
return.

— 16749

Early Mourning Hours

Your loving them does not leave them obliged to love you back.

16 and 18.

you were a persistent smiler and I, one of the reasons
behind it.

  days.

then came long nights filled with your grandparents'
memories, dreams that kept you from sleeping, your
conspiracy theories about "aliens and the government"
and secrets–I promised I'd keep them safe.

  weeks.

sometimes you were happy. we both lived off of the faith
we told each other to have. the laughter after all the tears
was the sweetest but the world was still too bitter to you,
who would never forgive yourself for not being good
enough for it.

  silence.

11 unanswered phone calls before I fell asleep waiting,
you were finally conscious enough to tell me you were
still alive. still at the hospital. still in need of prayers and
we felt it. how we felt it. the fear crawling down our
throats because you. you had enough for a successful
overdose.

months.

teenage eyes bustling with something we mistook for the
kind of love you told your mother about. but we meant
it. how we meant it. we felt the world at our fingertips
because all we needed was each other. you'd find some
place nice after the degree you'd have attained by the
time we were old enough for our parents to trust us and
maybe it'd be hard the first few months, but we'd be
alright. we'd be alright.

months.

the word "love" felt strange to my mouth and your name
was only glued to my lips by the dedication we
harboured towards a dream. our dream. we were both
busy in our own worlds but we checked into each other's
from time to time. met halfway. for the sake of it.

months.

I write about you for the sake of learning.

I hope they enjoy conspiracy files too and understand the
urgency in your sudden need to exit this place. that
person. whoever they may be.

Early Mourning Hours

when you finally find them; the one you will tell your
mother about and mean it when you say you're ready, I
will celebrate the victory of two teenagers who learned.
ran short of love and still managed to have faith in it. see
love. everywhere. express love. everywhere. and
understand the necessity of allowing it to form and break
when it wills.

the success of accepting that there are many soul mates.
that it was written we'd only need each other
for 16 and 18.

Early Mourning Hours

You were one of the most painful poems to write.

Early Mourning Hours

What happened to us was that

after many wonderful chapters together

(I will always treasure them)

you became the poems that were painful to write.

Early Mourning Hours

I want to be kind to myself.

I choose to accept the past and not revisit it except to take what I need from it as a lesson. To embrace the changes that have taken place however unexpected and difficult they may be.

I am grieving and letting go. Mourning as heavily as the weight of everything that ever felt authentic and left because it was free to leave. Mourning as deeply as the wounds have been made. I can stop my world only for so long. Life will move on and I must as well. I took a fall. That is okay. But to stay at rock bottom will only hurt me further. There is only the way up now. There is only the way out.

— Healing begins when you are willing to welcome
it inside

Early Mourning Hours

i.

I bite my bottom lip
respect the space you wanted.
I have swallowed so many words at your name
I am so full of it all. All I wish I could tell you.
You're but a thing of my past in the distance.
I am lost somewhere in between how it
doesn't have to be like this
and how maybe it does.
My love was. is. plentiful.
I uprooted my whole self for you.
Perhaps now I can
clear the vines
pluck the weeds
dig my nails back into my homeland.
Grow back into my self.
Relearn myself.

ii.

There is a fire beneath my ribcage and I don't know if it
is frustrated or desperate or mourning
(or everything at once).
The air around me has been heavy. Swelling with heat.
Unfriendly.

I think I have been burning my own heart alive.

Early Mourning Hours

iii.

and I kept those flowers for you

even after all this time

even after you left.

I still have to

walk a different path

with things that have your name written on them

find some water to clear the salt and cleanse this fire

pray for rain.

maybe you will return.

maybe you will not.

Early Mourning Hours

iv.

I hope there are clear skies

wherever you go

blue roses for you to love

moments of peace for you to find.

I hope there is

the kind of sleep that doesn't leave you so tired when

you wake

air that doesn't pull the dreams away from your

fingertips.

v.

and I still talk to our Lord about you.

do you feel it?

You will fall many times. Even after you have acknowledged this and begun to tread carefully, you will still fall. Each mishap is a lesson teaching you something. Sometimes we fail to learn, so it repeats itself. We notice the patterns but we don't heed their message and we get hurt. We are all hurt in some way. False smiles will not hold your tears back for long enough and those destructive habits you turn to when you worry, will only give you more to cry about. You need to be honest with yourself. You need to be that midnight-raw, in-depth conversation type of open with yourself and relearn what it is you fail to understand. Allow yourself to cry. Cry as much as it hurts. Pray as long as you've been crying for. And when you're finally able to stand up, fall to your knees for Him this time and pray again.

Allah (God) aids you even through His trials.

It has always been a lesson. He has always been guiding you, watching the progress that you never see yourself.

Early Mourning Hours

What's this, darling?
You've been chasing shadows
lost in the hope of being found
surrounded yet so alone.
And this, darling?
Constellations on your wrist.
You've been counting stars again
tracing wishes across your skin.
And darling
you know too well how to be silent in volumes
with those pure-hearted, sullen, stardust eyes.
Lonesome in your darkness with so much light to give.

My dear
you must be the moon.

Early Mourning Hours

You came across someone who took your genuine love for granted. After spending time in your heart, they left and took the home they built in it as well. They took pieces of you and they might not even look back and realise how much pain they've left you in later on. Perhaps you are hurt that a soul you cared for so much now seems indifferent towards your pain. Know that only goodness can come from the good you are. Maybe there were lessons both of you could take from experiencing one another hence they were sent your way. The mere fact that you went through it all is proof that you can handle what comes after it. Know that your precious heart is still brimming with love. It can heal perfectly within itself. It will heal. Sometimes we need to see just how much we are capable of giving, feeling, hurting and healing. Sometimes we need to be reminded of impermanence.

In due time, you will come to know the reason/s behind your experiences.

— you will heal

Early Mourning Hours

Tell your heart it is not silly, it is loyal.

It is not stubborn, it is forbearing.

It is not good for nothing, it is goodness-rich.

Tell your heart it is generous.

Profound.

Wondrous.

Splendid.

Say to it, *"My sweet love. I know how much you want to give, but we must save some of us for ourselves. We must be the receivers for a little while."*

Take it off of your sleeve.

Hold it closer to your chest.

Be alone with it, for a little while.

—— self care

Early Mourning Hours

Her arms were adorned with tattoos and she kept her
Quran close to her chest.

Her arms were adorned with tattoos and her hijab was
foreign to her skin.

Her arms were adorned with tattoos and she prayed the
afternoon prayer in her car.

People kept staring and
I could not keep my eyes off
her beautiful revolution.

Don't hide away my love.
They are incapacitated.
They do not know
the strength it takes
for you to be.

  — "the revert"

Early Mourning Hours

There is no veil between what I write
and what I mean to say.

——   honesty, the affliction.

Early Mourning Hours

I shy away from my Lord

dirt on my hands

my heart

my mouth

my mind.

Still

He beckons

for me to come closer

He knows what He has created

He is ever ready to shower me with mercy.

Early Mourning Hours

Some pains
they are not for you to understand
but to teach you the art of trusting
the reason behind your breath.

Early Mourning Hours

I cannot mourn the loss of us any longer.
I have travelled some distance away from myself to pay
my respects. It's time I return. I don't remember the
sound of my own voice.
We were too heavy for my heart to carry

so I laid us to rest.

But I kept the memories.
I'll keep our memories.

Early Mourning Hours

you broke me
but thank you for the poetry.

Early Mourning Hours

I will think of how well your favourite colour suits your skin tone. The sound of your laughter at its fullest. Your mother's voice. Your kindness toward strangers. The tears you cried for me. Your bad jokes. Your smile. I will think of the dreams we built. The love we invested into each other. The healing after so much pain. I will hear us sing together again. Talk our first conversation. See you walk into my life for the first time. I want to remember everything.

Everything except for the way you left.

To walk away does not necessarily mean to leave. To detach, does not mean to forget. You do not have to cut them out of your life, but you do not need to make them the centre of it either; this is where heartaches are born. We give power over ourselves to people who don't understand the magnitude of such love. We do not understand the magnitude of such love. The heart is already owned by a higher being. The Most High. Return it. Free yourself.

— ascension is to let go

Early Mourning Hours

The world could have turned against me.
I wouldn't have worried because I thought I had you to
turn to. You were my world. Perhaps that was my
mistake.

I decorated my skies with you–
my moon and stars altogether
and when you left
of course, darkness fell upon me.

Thank you.
How else would I have learned
to use my light for myself instead.
To need me.

Again
I looked to my Lord after turning away from Him
and still, He showed me the way out.
Kept me in His sight forever
when all I ever saw was you.

some time away

to meet the person I've become.

Early Mourning Hours

Unlearn the concept of
saving yourself by choosing
fire over water
hurting over healing
hardness over softness.

This is how the heart suffocates.
How there comes a time when
there is all the love in the world around you
but the wall you built stands solid
with the pain it clings to.

There is all the love in the world around you
and you aren't even able to inhale a single breath of it.

—   the love we breathe

Early Mourning Hours

You are not a lost cause

do you hear me.

You will be the light that your soul is brimming with.

You are someone's love.

Many people's love.

You are a body of hope.

A builder of dreams in more lives than just yours alone.

You are will and strength and the nerve to do everything

you were told you couldn't–whether it was the world or

your own mind that poisoned your heart with those

words.

You are full mutiny against the part of yourself that is

afraid to believe

because *you* believe. You do.

That is why you have fought and

why you will continue to fight.

Do you feel it?

The warmth.

Love

breathing in the pause between each sentence.

— letters to you

Early Mourning Hours

Even the poems have been struggling to hide their tears.

I think. Our parting was tragic indeed. Untimely, perhaps. Perhaps not. I know now, I will not loom over you like a past you want so badly to forget. I won't feel sorry for us anymore or shed tears over what we could've shared today. I know that I did not miss one opportunity to love you.

So I will remember you in this way:

We loved. And we loved well.

All I long for is simply that you remember me the same.

Early Mourning Hours

When they ask about you

what shall I say?

How can I pretend to not know you

as if your name was not written in my destiny

as if our mornings weren't filled with the sound of each

other's laughter

as if our nights were never spent consoling one another.

How can I forget your soul

when all the memories in me are still speaking of it.

You placed our past in my hand and walked away.

What can I do with it?

There is no shelf strong enough to hold the world we

shared

and my little heart is exhausted from carrying it inside.

(partly) why I am so tender?

i.

 I am simply always in love.

With her laugh and his kindness.

the rain. those clear blue skies

and the Mercy of the One Who created them.

ii.

The Love.

It floods my world

shakes it to the core.

Submerged.

I have been so full of it all

sometimes it is difficult to breathe.

Early Mourning Hours

your absence has taught me

love is just as

frightening

forgiving

forbearing

just as powerful

just as whole

even when it seems only one person

is giving it away all alone

i.

Our goodbyes

are sinking their way through my skin.

The heartache you are.

ii.

It is tragic how

we both loved so deeply

and so differently.

Even after God separated our paths

I gaze over my shoulder at you

and yearn for you to do the same.

iii.

Sometimes I catch myself running towards you.

I have to stop and whisper to my heart,

"Come back with me. Our Love will no longer turn to look at us."

Early Mourning Hours

My Lord
I denounce this world.
You are the sky my heart gazes upon during its sunset
and sunrise.
May the rains of Your mercy drench this body with Your
love, purify it
quench the unquenchable thirst of this traveller ever-
wandering distances away from the Beloved she seeks.
Sadness envelops this little heart and it knows no
salvation but You.
Do not deny me Your Light. In my own darkness, I
drown.
O Wish of one who desires
Who is there but You?
Who was there but You?
I sink deeper into desolation in this distance between us.
May I steal a glance at Your Light?

— i. Prayer

The day the Veil between You and me is lifted,

suffering will cease to exist even in memories long

forgotten.

O Answer of those who supplicate

will You spare a glance in my direction?

In this distance I dissipate.

Won't You remove the Veil?

Beloved

will You relieve me of this pain?

I denounce this world.

There is no cure but You.

— ii. Prayer

Our Lord is closer to us than we are to ourselves. If He chooses something for us, there is certainly nothing that would be better than His choice. He knows what we need before we realise it on our own. It's difficult to accept. It's difficult to comprehend–but He doesn't ask that of us. We are simply told to trust Him.

— Tawakkul

Lord, don't deny me the beauty of feeling Your
presence.
May the Veil between us be removed.
Forlorn.
My Beloved is so close
yet I am so far.

you'd still go back to them and heal with all your love
again if you got the chance. with your broken heart. with
your tired mind. a thousand times. you would.

—— the love you are

To be an endless fountain of love

regardless of how often it may

or may not rain.

How beautiful, yet painful.

How fulfilling, yet draining.

And I'll tell you;

the weather is always unpredictable.

i.

You've been such love to me.

Years and years of love.

ii.

We must not forget those who teach us how to love.

Those who stay with us when we give them reason to

leave. Show us just how beautiful we are. Mention our

names in sincere prayer. How can we forget theirs?

iii.

When your light is needed elsewhere

I will remember you.

In the sweet aftertaste of

"I love you."

Through the soft hues of flower petals.

In the scent of your favourite perfume.

During the first breath of evening air.

Your name will forever dance on each thread of memory

we share.

The child in me has been crying.

Perhaps I am tender because there are nights she spends

whispering her memories into my dreams.

I still love with her heart

and believe with her soul.

I care little for the fact that

someone

somewhere

could be searching for the love I have to offer.

If I do not accept the love I give

I will find no more happiness in anyone else

accepting it for me.

I must love the way I love first.

You caused me unimaginable pain.

I accept that now. I am not going to ignore my wound to excuse what happened between us for you. I will no longer do myself injustice. In order to heal I have to acknowledge that I am hurt–whether you will acknowledge it too or not. I will always value you as someone who's given me so many beautiful memories to treasure. Our separation feels untimely, but it is the decision you made so I will respect it.

And I will always love you, even if it's from afar.

Early Mourning Hours

Your love is so full of everything you need.

Please, for once, just give it to yourself.

Hold your own hand and build dreams for you.

For you.

Guard your own heart and build a home in it for you.

For you.

Line the edges of all its walls with love. the passages.

with love.

Kindle the firewood with love.

Dust the windows with love. the mirrors. with love.

Close the doors with love.

Trace a picket fence around the garden that grows

honey and waters salt and blooms flowers deeply rooted

into your heart. Welcome your self inside.

Close the curtains.

Forget where you leave the keys.

Send some letters out and

say you will return after a little while.

Know you will be healing and this home is for you.

Just for you.

i.
For how long can you wear your heart on your sleeve
until you wear it out.

ii.
Your love makes excuses to stay for people who'd never
do the same. I'm not going to ask you why it does that.
I'd like to know how. How can you love so much.

iii.
Silly, where did you find the audacity to love someone
who doesn't want you.

iv.
How could you do that to your heart.

v.
Was loving them easier than loving yourself.
Is that why you stayed.

vi.
Can a heart be in two minds as well.

— Unanswered

You haven't been sleeping lately. I wonder what thoughts you are staying up trying to catch. Which soul you are searching for.

"*We can wait for the sunrise together,*" I say. But your eyes–in front of me and distant and beautiful–are crying out for something else.

"*I will wait for the sun to rise while you wait for God,*" I say.

These days you keep your prayers short and spend more time staring at your palms in silence. You fall asleep waiting for yourself to finally ask whilst on your prayer mat. Your Lord? I think He continues to wait for you too.

Your mother told me that the soul travels to God when we sleep; I can only imagine how He must love for you to be with Him. You and your tender breathing. Your closed eyes and your soul that visits Him mid-prayer.

"*You should sleep earlier,*" I'd say. You ended up staring at the ceiling most nights.

And I thought you lost faith in prayers, but you treat the prayer mat as if it is the most comfortable place to leave your body.

Sometimes when you are pleading and crying and
screaming, when you are frustrated and sad and sick with
it all and He feels silent, you always think things you
don't mean.

I'm sure He has forgiven you. You say He is the Most
Merciful. And your mouth barely moves.

You grate your teeth as if chewing up the hope inside,
but your eyes still fog up with faith. You don't think you
can be forgiven. But I think it is you.

You, who cannot forgive your own self instead.

Your gaze meets mine. I have been staring for too long.
"You wait for the sun to rise, and I will wait for Allah.
We are both waiting to see light," you say.

You look faraway, and I know it is because you are
there—wherever you wanted to be.

You are lost in thought again, and I know it is because
you have found it—whatever you were looking for.

Early Mourning Hours

I wish you a patience so strong that it does not question
your pain.

Early Mourning Hours

I've long awaited my memories of our past to show
themselves.
Perhaps they are still mourning or
you took all of us with you the day you left.

I could write stories about us but
our love is a lost war between two whole countries
both sides grieving over burnt cities.
Neither of us knows exactly why but
our ships, that once shared the same course, now sail in
opposite directions.
You disappear into the distance a little more each time I
glance over my shoulder.
And your language used to roll off my tongue.
These days I barely remember its taste in my mouth.

Your footsteps are making their way out of my body.
From the soft of my lips. Through my eyes.
From my chest. Out my fingertips.
Lost at sea. I am searching for my homeland.
Perhaps it's best we leave, Love.
I am finding me.

Early Mourning Hours

Don't look for your answers in anyone. Your soul
already knows what you need. No one else can help you
better than you can help yourself.

Many a time it's best to seek silence on your own. Figure
yourself out. Grow into your skin again.
Sometimes silence is reassuring and
alone is comfortable.
Sometimes silence is agonising
and alone is frightening.
Try not to turn down good company and fresh air.

Kneel in humility, always. Allah will humble you from
every angle. Gradually. Life in its entirety is an
instrument of teaching.

Sometimes you're too hard on yourself, you really are. If
you feel hurt, then acknowledge your wound. If you
need time to heal, take time to heal. You're tender.
Gentle skinned, hearted and all.
You can take pain without stopping to catch your breath
only for so long.

There is love all around. It may take different forms, but it is still sincere. Wholehearted. Don't ignore it because it didn't live up to your expectations at some stage. Don't trample over other hearts because your own heart is sore. That is unfair.

The small bit of faith you've been clinging to, it will do you good. It won't fail you. Allah is your *Maula* [Protector]. Your *Wakeel*. [Trustee]

— what the pain taught me

Early Mourning Hours

When their presence

in your heart

was finally accompanied

by their being

at your side

it somehow felt no different

to their absence.

—— this is how you will know

Early Mourning Hours

I cannot end your hardship

nor can I stop your tears from falling.

I can cradle your sadness

and embrace you with my prayers.

I can love you

but I cannot save you.

I will love you.

That is all I know how to do.

Gone are the days

of monsters

that live

beneath our beds.

Now, there are those

dwelling in the past

and anticipating

the future,

monsters

that lurk

inside of our heads.

— transition

It is only when trials
create obstacles along our paths
only when pain has us fall
that we seem to
land upon faith.

— to rise is to have fallen

Sometimes we think we find ourselves in someone when really, we just find pieces of them that we learn to love and agree with. We adopt those pieces and inculcate their characteristics into our own habits. We make parts of them our own and when they leave, we're just left with those pieces we took—whether they're healthy or not. We don't know what to do with them besides reminisce over the person they belong to. We hang onto them because they're the only thing we have left of someone so beloved to us.

You are holding onto a past, onto what was. By doing so, you avoid acknowledging what is meant to be at this very moment; if it is a life that is currently devoid of them, then so be it. It is time for you to loosen your grasp on what does not belong to you and grab hold of something that does: *yourself.* It is time to rediscover yourself.

To find company within your own company.
To accept the present for what it has become, along with the many different pieces you have left of you. They make up the whole person you are now.

"It's been a while," I said, hovering my pen over the page.

"*Talk to me,*" the page answered.

"I don't know how to."

- "S*peak as you did those many times before.*"

"I was a different person then."

- "*Your soul is the same.*"

"Where do I begin?"

- "*What has changed?*"

Early Mourning Hours

She was a heartbreak

staring back at me with those big brown eyes.

I describe myself
as abundance
a soul overflowing
I am not able to *be*
in moderation
My love comes in tides
and my jealousy burns
My sadness pours
and my anger rages
I can destroy merely by being
I spend days rescuing my self
from natural disaster.

Early Mourning Hours

Tonight I am in darkness surviving off the sombre glow of these stars alone. Tonight, I am small and the world is too vast to consider this humbled being. This search for guidance has rendered me unnerved. Unheard. I am screaming, from my lungs through my eyes and I know I am not loud enough. I am gentle. I am excruciatingly soft. This wind will travel skies carrying my cry to the heavens and I will still be waiting for You to answer me, my Lord. I cannot hear You or see You or feel You in this moment, however long this moment may last, but I believe. Fiercely.

You are listening
and I will wait.

—— Night-Long Lament: Contemplation and Prayer

My love is blatant.

It is brutally honest.

I spend nights

cradling my heart

mothering it

lulling it to sleep

after coming home to me in tears

from a world that punishes it

for speaking the truth.

Letting go of them will be difficult. Loosening your grip off the rope of dreams you held to so tightly will sting your palms but ultimately, nothing will feel better than leaving something that does not belong to you, in return for something that does. Night's darkness will disappear. The sun will rise. Those scars will heal along with your aching heart. We hurt, we learn, and we move on.

Choose light.

Let it consume your shadows

expand

become so excruciatingly bright

it no longer has to confront your darkness.

Overtake.

— feed your positive energy

Early Mourning Hours

Lord can You hear me

Lord can You hear me

Lord can You hear me

Lord please hear me

I know You are listening

I know You have heard every tear and witnessed every

pain. That pain. my trials. my errors. my hardships.

Those pains. these pains. the pains You have given me.

I am struggling I am struggling I am struggling I am

struggling.

I am struggling to keep up with how

they run from day to day to day to day to day to day to

day to day.

Today, I feel slow.

My faith

is running

out of time.

I believe in You I believe I believe I believe I believe.

I believe You.

Help me believe in myself too.

Early Mourning Hours

Light rain tapped softly at my window this morning.
He woke me up to partake of His Mercy.

—   Fajr (the early morning prayer)

Early Mourning Hours

I want to hold on as tightly as I have been, but these palms are scarred. This heart is tired and these wounds will only deepen. There was love. There is love. But love is the only place wherein our story can continue, for to each other; we have ended. You were lesson upon lesson for me. I will cherish everything I've learnt. It's difficult, leaving what could have been. Maybe someday I will walk back to us, or you will, or together we may both cross paths once again. Perhaps we will be different. Better. Ready. Perhaps we will be ready for what we thought would become of us. If the divine knot that tied our destinies together is beginning to loosen, I will prepare myself for it to untie us. Believe me, I have fought for it not to. But our time is passing. We are passing, in different directions. The love we share will always stay, but we cannot dwell within it. Where we stand is in transition from what was, to what must be. Take my sweet memories with you.

I will always carry yours along with me.

Detaching yourself from someone doesn't mean feeling nothing at all for them. We're sensitive beings, not emotionless vessels. Keeping a few memories of someone does not make you weak. Actually detaching yourself entails accepting that they might never even be in your life again, except for the few precious moments that will always reside within your heart. It means being at peace with the past you have with them and acknowledging a present without them. You are always going to feel a certain way about someone who's touched your heart. It's up to you to decide whether that will continue to bring you a sense of pain or a sense of peace instead.

Early Mourning Hours

father

I try so much harder

to fit into your shoes and

my path is worlds apart from yours.

perhaps my feet ache because

they do not belong to the son you might have had

but how can you ignore the way the sound of our

footsteps echo one another.

Early Mourning Hours

When you want to heal
you must keep your distance from
what causes damage:

those things. at night.
the glass you broke.
kitchen knives.
lighters.
liquor.

high ways. freeways.
and that dark alley.
old photographs.
that perfume.
pills. and
people.

(as long as it takes)

Early Mourning Hours

i.

Get up.

Open some curtains

the windows too.

The light will hurt for a few moments

even the evening glow off the glass

can pain slightly.

Inhale

exhale

inhale

exhale

you're doing it

almost

steady.

Listen to the birds

the cars

anything that is busy with life.

Soon that will be you as well

there on the outside and

not held captive by your mind all

confined within your living space

where help will not look for you.

ii.

Spring clean

even if it's winter.

Have your favourite cereal

at night or

hours of the morning when it is

too early to make any sounds.

Step outside

visit the flowers

and nurture

with the same love you yearn for.

It will come for you

after it has come from you.

iii.

Get up.

Wash off the nightmares clinging to your skin

from the day before yesterday.

Look into the mirror.

Eyes sunken. Tired. Raging.

Red from the war.

They have been cleansing

and cleansing

and cleansing.

Give them a break.

Let water clear the salt.

iv.

Write

un.write the pain

Draw

un.draw the pain

Sing

un.sing the pain

Talk

un.talk the pain

Pray

and heal

v.

Your body is tired of struggling.

Tired of fighting itself

and physical pain killers for

wounds that are spiritual. Emotional.

Exercise your prayer and art

(whatever they may be).

Build. Strengthen your self.

Spiritually.

Emotionally.

   — tend

Even if you leave

you will not be absent.

I wear you in my writing

you are the ink

etched onto pages

and hearts.

— muse

Early Mourning Hours

How much longer will it take to

undo your laugh from my eyes

brush your touch out of my skin

unlearn your voice

every night before I sleep.

I am struggling let you go.

To leave something that became such a big part of me

feels like losing me altogether

but I will loosen my grip.

I am hidden somewhere in between our separation.

The sky will part to reveal the moon

and I will soft-glow until I find myself amidst the

darkness.

— u|s

The challenge is not in fixing them. It is in accepting that no matter how much love you try to mend with, their condition will only change when they truly want it to. That they haven't acknowledged the same pain you see in them. That it is between them and their Lord and your love will soothe the oceans in them, but only He possesses the power to help them save themselves from drowning.

Early Mourning Hours

Sometimes you are alone with your thoughts. The walls
cave in and your head throbs from the pressure of
holding in your cries. You feel yourself fall deeper, but
forget that your troubles are not bottomless. Soon you
are going to land. And when you do, know that you are
able to climb up again. God heard the many prayers your
heart whispered to Him. Remember that you need only
ask, and you will receive your answer. Be it in the form
of a person's entrance, departure, or perhaps your will to
stay. The rising of the morning's sun; your survival to
the next day. A door opening, a door closing, or simply a
sudden peace in the silence as you exhale the past night
away. It will come.
With hardship, comes ease.

— ii." *with* "

You're forever tearing yourself apart for not being able
to piece yourself back together quickly enough
hating yourself whilst loving them you
fork your soul out onto silver platters and expect your
being to be nourished with the leftovers you feed it after
they've left you
burning your walls at the edges hoping to rise from
whatever is left of you when you are not a phoenix you
are so much more at times ash and others risen but most
importantly
you are human.
you are your home.
stop destroying it and arriving to a vacancy at the end of
the day
stop selling it out and evicting yourself from your own
heart
rebuild.
brick by brick take hold of you
alone does not mean lonely it means you hide away the
"*welcom*e" doormat because you don't need guests right
now.
you are undergoing a reconstruction of all the pieces
you've deconstructed in order to build someone else

Early Mourning Hours

have them wait outside for a bit
how can you help rebuild others when you have nothing
left of yourself to use

let your eyes greet light like the windowpane that faces
the East every sunrise
steps of patience from floors of faith right up to a rooftop
of resilience
walls thick enough to withstand the storm from inside
too.
you don't need the *"welcome"* doormat right now.
you need you.

— guesthouse

Patience.

Goodness will spring from our pain.

Flowers will blossom from these wounds.

It will take time

as beautiful things do.

— things to tell a heart at night

Early Mourning Hours

these letters I write

these prayers on my lips

this pain in my heart and

the love inside it as well.

they are yours.

Early Mourning Hours

The love letters written in your eyes.

Who are they addressed to?

Early Mourning Hours

We were not of the same skin

nor were our ancestors of the same kin.

We loved different lands

yet in each other

found common grounds.

Our homes became one another.

Unapologetically

each heartbeat for you

and every heartbeat for me

conspired against history.

Love is our nationality.

Early Mourning Hours

Don't be ashamed

that you have

embodied

the sun's light

and your tongue

resonates

with the land

of your ancestors.

— melanin

Early Mourning Hours

I don't hide the pain in my voice.
I am not afraid of my vulnerability or
the intimacy of eye contact between tears.
This is my strength.

    —   soft powers

can you feel it.

the gravity.

the slow pull of us deeper into one another

yet further away from each other.

my hands are still tugging at your clothes.

holding fiercely

fighting to keep

but you cease to stay.

I pray I am hidden somewhere within your destiny.

I will weep over memories of you.

cradle them in my arms

for the eternity between our departure and return.

holding you like this has been selfish.

your dreams are elsewhere.

you are still in front of me and

I miss you already.

We are simply needed elsewhere.

— until we meet again

Your soul mate. Whichever soul mate they are.

Your closeness to them can be the same thing that breaks you apart if you let go of yourself and Allah, Who made it possible, in order to hold more tightly onto them.

It is when attachments break you away from your own self that you realise you need some distance. To reconnect, reclaim. You *do* know it, because you feel pain more often than love. You don't have to leave them. Distance does not mean leave. We need space to breathe. To move. It only scares us because we interpret it all as loss.

Love will find ways to be with you.

Wherever, whenever needed.

Right now

you are needed by you.

You are in need of Him

and this calling, you cannot ignore.

—   this closeness can be the same thing that tears
     you apart

Early Mourning Hours

This is not the life you are capable of.

Early Mourning Hours

If in the end
you became closer to your Lord,
know that it all happened to bring you back to Him
and pull you back into
yourself.

Early Mourning Hours

Where are you my Lord

and where am I.

Are we close

or am I lost

far, far away from You.

I think of You

and I am ashamed that You are in my mind

but not my words

and you are in my heart

but not my actions.

You are everywhere

but I am ashamed because

I don't feel worthy of having You near me

and You *are* near me but I am ashamed that

I have not made an effort to be near You too.

what am I to do

when your words are harsh

and my petal skin begins to bruise.

      — do speak gently, please

Early Mourning Hours

We were both outgrowing the warm houses we built in
each other's hearts.

Early Mourning Hours

And perhaps one day

someone you love will

break your heart too.

And you'll be more shattered than ever before.

More miserable. more poetic. red-eyed. tender. early

morning hours and

questioning of destiny

than ever before.

And perhaps on quiet nights when they might remember

your name or

the way you made them laugh

just like me, you will think to yourself

that if given the chance; you would give up all your

beautiful poetry simply to relive the past you shared with

them.

Perhaps reminding yourself how they left you isn't going

to change the fact that you stayed.

You'd still let go for them in a single heartbeat.

even if it's a broken one.

even your broken one.

Early Mourning Hours

Don't look for yourself in someone else.
Don't search for your love in their heart
or your kindness in their eyes
or your sincerity in their voice
or your understanding in their mind.
Don't think you've found yourself in someone
to become disappointed when one day you see
their soul
instead of a reflection of your own.

The thing about the ending.

You can taste it coming weeks before. You will spend nights subconsciously strengthening your heart for the break, but find later on that no amount of preparation can ease the pain. Everything (even the good things) leads up to the moment you catch yourself falling to the bathroom floor. And months later you might still feel the heat of tears warm your eyes when you hear of them. Accidently pick their favourite colour. Eat their favourite food. Your heart will hurt just a little bit. Breathe a little deeper than usual. Maybe you still remember them in your prayers. If you are tender. If you do not hate. Even then you will wonder why things had to turn out the way they did. But neither of you could help it. Perhaps it was tragic. And you were irreplaceable to each other. Inseparable. But you are separated now and my love, looking back in that direction with those eyes and those memories; that will only hurt you more.

Make peace with the past. Make peace with its pain.
Welcome in the healing by acknowledging that the
wounds are there in the first place. Be kind to yourself.
Be kind to the ones who hurt you. Be the love you need
for yourself. And when you are healed, be the love that
others may need as well.

So you try to change things that don't need to be
changed.

Fix what was never broken.

Take a different path, unknowingly forsaking the perfect
one you were following.

Your fears are controlling your actions.

Your fears are controlling your actions, and it's never
too late to admit so.

To take a step back, look at the road you wanted to
travel.

Maybe even choose it again.

Early Mourning Hours

My Lord

I await the day that I ascend.

My Beloved

this heart is absent from You

and yearns to feel Your presence.

My Light

what an honour You have bestowed upon the skies.

The Heavens forever witness the sight of You

and perhaps one day

I will too.

— i. Lament

Early Mourning Hours

If my soul could only remember how it felt
to be fashioned by You.
Those who reside in the Heavens
tell me
what is the presence of my Lord like?
And the mountains that crumbled before His Majesty
how is His Light?
O Moon, tell me, are you closer to His Throne than I am
to it?
You might be, but He is closer to me than the blood
beneath my skin.
And my Lord sees me, hears me, knows me.
Still. I yearn only for a glimpse of Him.

— ii. Lament

It's taken years of reclaiming

reclaiming pieces of my heart for me to realise

that it is mine to keep.

It's taken years of rebuilding

rebuilding pieces of myself for me to realise

that I am my own home to return to at the end of the day.

None of me is meant to be given away.

Early Mourning Hours

I have fought long and hard for you.
It is time for me to pick my heart up and leave.

Early Mourning Hours

the light in me is tired.

What kind of honour is he able to hold while his hands
are covered in his daughter's blood?

What kind of honour is he able to hold while his hands
are covered in his sister's blood?

What kind of honour is he able to hold while his hands
are covered in his wife's blood?

What kind of honour

is he able to hold

while the blood

of a woman

still flows through his veins and

the very bone he is grown from

is cursing him.

— "honour" killings.

Early Mourning Hours

Will we watch on as history rewrites the same stories,
each time using the language of a different nation.
When the sun finally rises, will we realise that whilst
waiting for better days to come, we abandoned our
neighbours during their darkest hours.
The sky may weep with us, but all our tears will not
wash away the blood stains we've left on the streets.

Early Mourning Hours

How do you grow

torn from your motherland

planted in soil cultivated by the blood,

sweat and tears of your people.

And if you leave, where will you go?

This place is home now.

And if you leave, where will you go?

To a mother who is foreign to you

and you to her?

Although your tongue is screaming

to answer her call

she does not understand you.

You no longer understand her.

Will you ever return

to the mother you do not know?

And how will you stay

in this new land

this home

that does not want you either.

— immigrant

Early Mourning Hours

I pull the love out of my chest
and lay it at your doorstep.
Time might have you forget
whose footsteps are walked across your heart
whose roses are scattered throughout your memories
whose touch is traced across your skin.
One day I may leave, but you will be healed
and you will nurture someone else.

Early Mourning Hours

In my efforts to have you love me back
with the kind of love I gave to you
I abandoned myself
in pursuit of something
I could only ever find within.
Your eyes might never look at me as sincerely
as mine do when I look at you.
Your words might never sound as loving to my ears
as mine do when I let them gently slip off my lips.
Perhaps my touch was always more tender.
I have chased after you and
somewhere in the blur of my hopes
lost sight of us both.
I must find myself again.

— reclaim

Early Mourning Hours

There is no shame in expecting reciprocation.

Seeking balance is natural.

You must understand that not everyone's heart is so
full of love
that they'd be willing to return yours the way you let
them receive it.

Early Mourning Hours

How many more lives will you invest yourself in?

Break your self into pieces to leave with them

and when the time comes for you to bloom

through a pain of your own,

you have nothing left to fuel your growth.

Not a slither of light left for you to flourish in.

You too are worth the love you spend on everyone else.

Early Mourning Hours

I cry out to The Beloved
Stand near me!
While inscribed in His Holy Book is
"*He is with you wherever you may be.*"

Yet I feel so far

so I cry out to The Beloved
Hold me closer within You!

But as I remember The Beloved within myself
The Beloved remembers me too.

Still I feel forsaken

so I cry out to The Beloved
Take me into Your Hands!
While there my soul remains safely kept
as it was when eternity began.

I decided to allow my heart to let go of its grief and hope
for lovers who have left and lovers who have yet to
arrive.

My chest was emptied and for a moment
there was nothing felt
until the sight of My Beloved entered into it.

The Veil lifted, I felt His Light
and I knew then
I had finally come home.

    —— Surrender.

Writing is a vulnerable, honest place. I go there to listen to what my soul has to say. Hear the depths of my heart every now and then. Meet my self over and over again, and each time, it is as if I am visiting a stranger. Consoling the stranger. Loving the stranger. Each time, I am reading her words as if they were not written by my own hand. Some stories I recognise, some I don't. I see poems that look like my past but don't feel familiar. And I see poems that shake my name out from deep beneath my skin.

—— Samihah

Early Mourning Hours

Sometimes I lose myself
only to stumble upon me
along paths that lead to my Lord.
I feel comfort in knowing
that wherever You are,
O Allah,
I am there too.

Early Mourning Hours

In a world where we are always chasing things;
people, places, our own shadows.
Faith is all we can really hold onto
when even our own dreams seem out of reach.

Do you remember what it feels like
to breathe again.
More than inhaling, exhaling.

With each sigh,
the pain of the past is forgiven, accepted
and leaves with your breath.

Early Mourning Hours

I cry my mother's tears.

I am the softest, strongest thing I know.

I will love because I know what it feels like to not receive love. I will be kind because I know what it feels like to not be treated kindly when it's most needed. I will forgive as much as I seek forgiveness. I will convey the lessons I learn because there were many times I needed wisdom and wasn't able to find it easily. I will be generous with my goodness — not because I am good, but because it is fulfilling. Pouring out to others will not leave me empty because I have learnt to pour back into myself. Times come when I am able to pick sweet fruits off the seeds I have sown. Yes, my heart has felt as if it had been punctured by thorns. I have been entangled in my own sadness many times before. It was tempting to cage my emotions the way the world says I should, but I grew flowers with them instead. At the peak of your pain, you can become the very person or thing that caused it and hurt everyone else, or you can choose to use it to strengthen yourself. You can navigate it. Take back your heart from what is hurting it. Retreat into yourself for however long you need to be away. Feel so that you may heal.

Early Mourning Hours

I will decorate the places I find myself in with love.
Kindness. Wisdom. Goodness. That is needed. Very
much needed.

— in times of pain

I said to my body,
"It was never your fault
all you did was love
all you do is love."

Early Mourning Hours

I held my heart in my hands
and apologised for the hurt,
"I am going to love you and love you in
all the ways I should have a long time ago."

Made in the USA
Columbia, SC
20 July 2020

14171799R00086